This book is a collection of affirmations for children. As children grow and develop they form opinions about themselves through the words and actions of other people. Parents who practice and implement the use of affirmations empower their children to create positive thought patterns and influence behavioral changes for the better. Affirmations are statements that we say to ourselves that can shift our mindset. The more we repeat positive thoughts, the easier we can recall them later. Affirmations can motivate action, promote concentration on goals, change negative thought patterns into positive ones, influence the subconscious mind to access new beliefs and boost self-confidence.

Dedicated to My Children:

Our Deepest Fear

Our deepest fear is not that we are inadequate.
Our deepest fear is that we are powerful beyond measure.
It is our light not our darkness that most frighten us.
We ask ourselves, who am I to be brilliant, gorgeous, talented and
fabulous? Actually, who are you not to be?
You are a child of God.
Your playing small does not serve the world.
There's nothing enlightened about shrinking so that other people won't
feel insecure around you.
We are all meant to shine, as children do.
We were born to make manifest the glory of God that is within us.
It's not just in some of us; it's in everyone.
And as we let our own light shine, we unconsciously give other people
permission to do the same.
As we are liberated from our own fear,
Our presence automatically liberates others.

-Marianne Williamson

I am
Strong
and
Determined

I
Choose
my
Attitude

Today
is going to be a
Good Day

I
Try
New Things

I am Grateful

I
am
Ready to Learn

Today
is a
Fresh Start

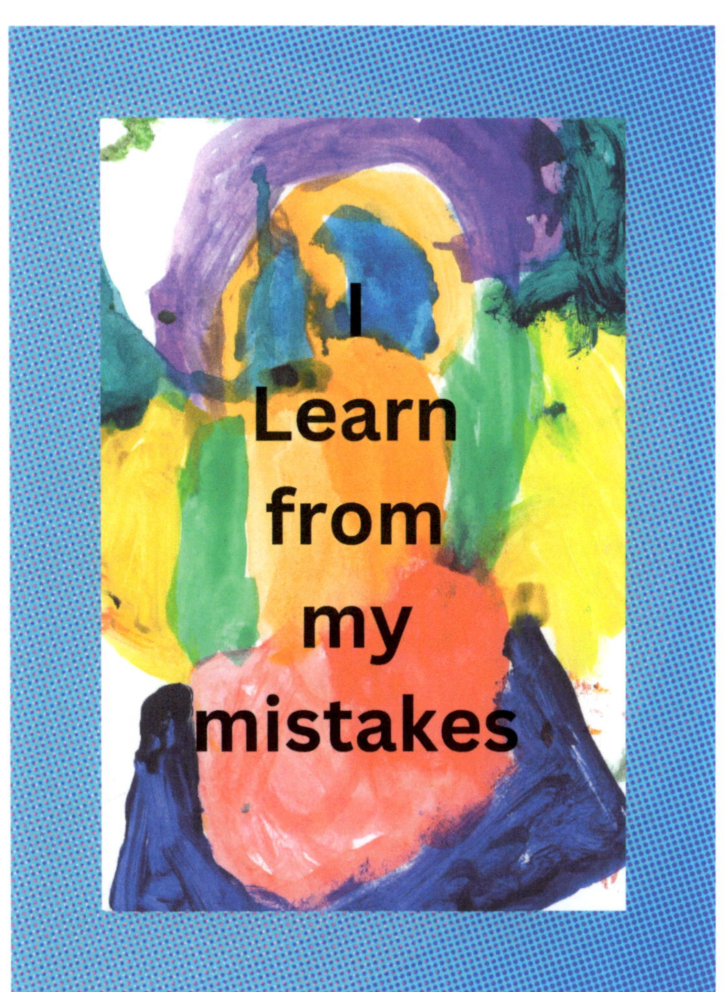

I
Learn
from
my
mistakes

I
Do My
Best

I am
A Great Listener

There is only
One Me

I Never give up

My
Challenges
help
me Grow

All of
my
Problems
have
Solutions

I
get
Better
Every
Single
Day

I have
the
Confidence
to be
Myself

I am
Prepared
to be
Successful

I
Like
Myself
for who
I am

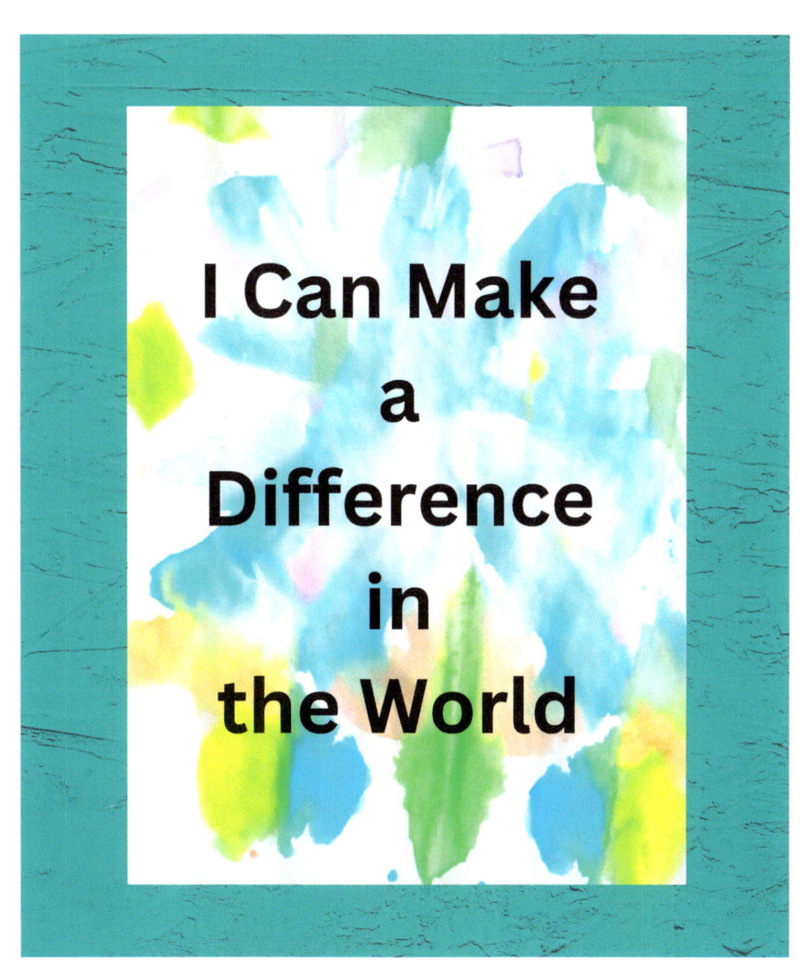

I Can Make
a
Difference
in
the World

No
Matter
How hard
it is
I
Can
Do It